Counting by: Tens

Esther Sarfatti

Rourke
Publishing LLC
Vero Beach, Florida 32964

www.rourkepublishing.com

PHOTO CREDITS: © Nicole S. Young: title page; © Perry Correll: page 3; © Renee Brady: pages 5 and 9;
© Angelika Stern: page 7; © Bart Broek: page 11; © Rob Sylvan: page 13; © Tim McCaig: page 15;
© Aleksandr Lobanov: page 17; © Arturo Limon: page 19.

Editor: Robert Stengard-Olliges

Cover design by Nicola Stratford.

Library of Congress Cataloging-in-Publication Data

Sarfatti, Esther.
  Counting by : tens / Esther Sarfatti.
     p. cm. -- (Concepts)
  ISBN 978-1-60044-522-4 (Hardcover)
  ISBN 978-1-60044-663-4 (Softcover)
  1. Counting--Juvenile literature. I. Title.
   QA113.S356 2008
   513.2'11--dc22
                                      2007014036

Printed in the USA

CG/CG

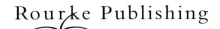

Rourke Publishing

www.rourkepublishing.com – rourke@rourkepublishing.com
Post Office Box 3328, Vero Beach, FL 32964

This is ten.

What comes in tens?

Ten

10

10

Ten

Ten

10

5

The crab has ten legs.

The table has ten lunch bags.

9

You have ten fingernails.

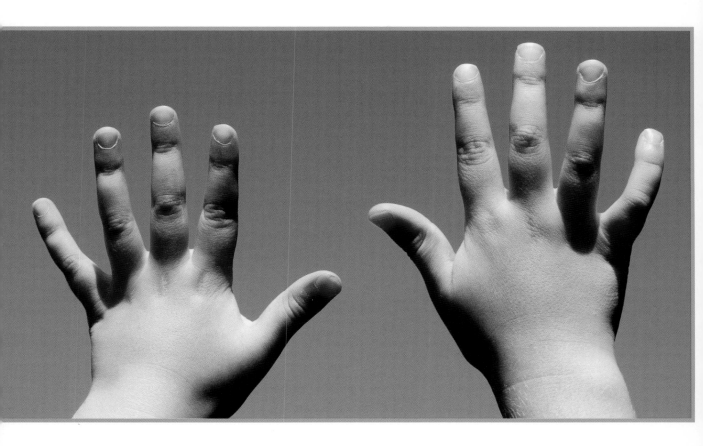

11

This flock has ten birds.

12

13

This candy cane has
ten big stripes.

15

This is ten pencils.

17

This flower has ten petals.

This is ten pennies.

1¢   1¢   1¢   1¢   1¢

1¢   1¢   1¢   1¢   1¢

These ten penguins are sliding. Counting by tens is fun!

Index

birds   12
crab   6
lunch bags   8
pencils   16

Further Reading

Dahl, Michael. *Ants at the Picnic: Counting by Tens*. Picture Window Books, 2006.

Dahl, Michael. *Bunches of Buttons: Counting by Tens*. Picture Window Books, 2006.

Trumbauer, Lisa. *Qué hace diez/What Makes Ten?*. Yellow Umbrella Books, 2006.

Recommended Websites

www.edhelper.com/kindergarten/Number_10.htm
www.enchantedlearning.com/books/howmany/10/

About the Author

Esther Sarfatti has worked with children's books for over 15 years as an editor and translator. This is her first series as an author. Born in Brooklyn, New York, and brought up in a trilingual home, Esther currently lives with her husband and son in Madrid, Spain.